23 Tips To Survive A Long Flight (As A Passenger)

by

James Nixon

CrammondMEDIA
ISBN: 978-0-9944760-7-4 (paperback)

Excellent Advice!

After a thirty year aviation career, I still got ripped-off on a recent charter flight to Mexico.

Who knew that investing an extra $50 for a "premium" front seat would mean sitting beside the toilet lineup for five hours —with someone's butt at my head level!

James' thoughtful and informative tips will enable you to avoid many such pitfalls and a few far more serious ones, even if you've been flying for decades.

- I. Hunt (Retired A380 Captain)

First published by CrammondMEDIA in 2017

Copyright ©CrammondMEDIA2018

The moral right of the author has been asserted.

All rights reserved. No part of this book may be reproduced or transmitted by any person or entity, including internet search engines or retailers, in any form or by any means, electronic or mechanical, including photocopying (except under the statutory exceptions provisions of the Australian *Copyright Act 1968*), recording, scanning, or by any information storage and retrieval system without the prior written permission of the principal of CrammondMEDIA.

National Library of Australia
Cataloguing-in-Publication entry

Creator: Nixon, James, 1959- author.

Title: **23 tips to survive a long flight : as a passenger** / by James C Nixon.

ISBN: 9780994476074 (paperback)

Notes: Includes bibliographical references and index.

Subjects: Air travel--Guidebooks.

Air travel--Psychological aspects
Air travel--Safety measures.
International travel--Guidebooks.
International travel--Psychological aspects.

Amazon: https://www.amazon.com/dp/B074N3TPL3

Website: www.jamesnixon.com

Text: 1st January 2018 (Ingrams version)

NOTE: The 23Tips started as a bonus chapter in *Sleeping For Pilots & Cabin Crew (And Other Insomniacs)*. If you already have that book, save your money!

Legal Disclaimer

The views expressed by the Author are his own.

The information provided within this book is for general informational purposes only. While we try to keep the information correct, there are no representations or warranties, express or implied, about the completeness, accuracy, reliability, suitability or availability with respect to the information, products, services, contained in this book for any purpose. Any use of this information is at your own risk.

Various paragraphs in this book have used information from the official investigation sources, articles appearing on both the internet and in the media. Correct attribution and links to the source material are given. If you can find any paragraph where correct attribution has not been given, advise us, and we will make amendments to subsequent editions.

The author, his agent and publisher do not have any control, warrant the performance, effectiveness or applicability of sites listed or linked-to in this book or use by any third party of this book's content, through any physical or electronic medium or of such third party's content and opinion. All links and references in this book are for information purposes only and are not warranted for content, accuracy or other implied or explicit purpose.

While the author has made every effort to ensure that the information in this book was correct at the time of publication, neither the author, his agent nor the publisher assume any responsibility for errors, or for changes that occur after publication.

The Author, its agent and publisher, to the fullest extent permitted by law hereby disclaim any liability to any party for any expense, loss, damage, physical or mental anguish or disruption caused by the statements, opinion, errors or omissions, whether such errors or omissions result from negligence, accident, or any other cause.

No part of this book may be reproduced or transmitted in any form or by any means, electronic or mechanical, including photocopying, recording or by any information storage and retrieval system, without written permission from the author. Direct all enquiries to:

Kerryn@CrammondMedia.com

©**CrammondMEDIA2018**

Foreword

Living in probably the most beautiful country on earth has one major disadvantage. We are a long way from England, Europe and the United States, places which we nevertheless have an insatiable urge to visit. However, Australians take on the challenge with an enthusiasm which astounds our American and British friends. My husband and I have done many long haul flights with a number of different airlines.

Captain James Nixon's book *"23 Tips to Survive a Long Haul Flight (as a passenger)"* contains a wealth of information as to how to make long haul flights a more manageable and pleasant experience. He knows the airline industry and it's that knowledge which he brings to this book. It is essential reading for the novice flyer. We wish that it had been in existence some forty years ago when we first started to travel internationally.

For seasoned travelers James' summary check list is particularly useful for those of us who think we might know it all … but don't!

James writes in the same easy to read style as he does in *"Sleeping for Pilots and Cabin Crew"* and in his intriguing book *"The Crash of*

MH370". His anecdotes are from the real experiences of sometimes very unfortunate passengers. And yes, it is very easy to make a mistake when booking online and an airline's safety record is more important reading than the meal service menu. Take the time before you fly to select your seat.

  Read the book, act on its recommendations and then sit back and enjoy your flight!

    Lynette M Hallett
    Seasoned Traveller

Introduction

A wise old aviation medical examiner sat looking thoughtfully, then raised his head. In his thick Welsh accent he proclaimed:
'The granny you put onto a plane in London is NOT the same little old lady who gets off the plane in Melbourne.'

Long haul flying wears you out, regardless of the direction and time zones crossed, if any, and then jet lag knocks you around afterward. How can you make the flight less harrowing so you can have a better experience before, during and after the flight?

Throughout my flying career, and particularly during the thirteen and half years working overseas, I lost count of the number of times people asked how I handled the long haul flights.

When you are the captain, it is fairly easy: no one puts their seatback in your lap in the cockpit, you spend time in the bunk on the really long flights, and jet lag doesn't often affect you since you are back in your own bed in a few days.

But the delights of staff travel, and traveling back and forth to your home country, mean that you soon develop skills as a passenger.

What makes it worse is hearing horror stories from your friends who neglected to ask for tips before embarking on their "World Discovery Tour" — 20 countries in 21 days. If only they had asked.

This short guide started as a bonus chapter to *"Sleeping For Pilots & Cabin Crew (And Other Insomniacs)"* and has grown into a full checklist of things to do to lessen the effects of long haul travel.

Feel free to drop me an email if you have any other tips and we will share them in future editions. After all, we need to help each other out when trying to make it through those long, boring flights.

James Nixon
January 2018

Table Of Contents

1. The Reason We Fly — 1
2. The Right Airline — 5
3. Passport — 9
4. Visas — 11
5. Travel Agent — 13
6. Earplugs & Eyeshades — 17
7. Frequent Flier — 21
8. Credit Card & Lounges — 25
9. Travel Insurance — 29
10. Meals, Seats, Online Check-In — 31
11. Audiobooks — 33
12. Change The Channel — 37
13. Jet Lag — 39
14. Deal With the Fear — 59
15. Socks — 63
16. Plan Ahead — 65
17. Doctor — 67
18. Hypoxia / Nicotine — 69
19. Pack Cleverly — 73
20. Get There Early — 77
21. Enjoy The Airport — 79
22. On The Aircraft — 85
23. The Approach & Landing — 89

The Checklist — **93**

What's Next? — 97
Acknowledgements — 99
Sleeping For Pilots & Cabin Crew — 101
The Crash Of MH370 — 109
Endnotes — 117

1. The Reason We Fly

Having been in the game for over thirty years, it is sad to look back and see the "de-aviation" of the flying experience. Nowadays when we push-back into our own exhaust fumes and that marvelous kerosene smell fills the cabin, we can guarantee a worried call from the cabin crew advising us of the fumes. When we were kids, we used to go to airports to sniff the kerosene on the breeze. The Jet-A1 got into our blood and we became aviators.

Today the terminal is air-conditioned and the aerobridge/jetbridge is fireproofed; guaranteed to prevent the ingestion of flames or fumes from the tarmac. And now most people couldn't tell you what brand of aircraft they were in until they had read the safety card. And that is if they read it at all.

It is all about marketing, destinations, saving money, collecting points, watching movies and having a "restaurant experience." Why? Because the airlines don't want you to think about what, in fact, is really happening.

Only meters away, there is a blast furnace or two, white hot metal spinning within a few centimeters of a swimming pool full of volatile fuel. The takeoff roll sees you going faster than a formula one car, and then it starts to speed up. You are doing 500 kph (310 mph) in minutes.

In the cruise, the air is so cold; only a few centimeters from your face, that you would snap freeze. You are going so fast that the wind would strip off your clothes, and if you opened your mouth, your skin too. The engine noise would deafen you.

There haven't been recent studies, but in 2007, the New York Times reported that the American National Institute of Mental Health had put the number of Americans who suffered 'aviophobia' at 6.5%[1] Yet a broader study done in Australia during the early 1980s reflected that half the general public was 'too scared to fly.' Whatever the real figure, the concept of flying is stressful for a percentage of people. The physics involved is beyond the understanding of nearly all the passengers and most of the people who work for the airline. Yet they roll up on the jetbridge, eager to get on.

Or do they?

On every flight there are terrified travelers, first-time fliers, people fleeing a horrible past, grandparents looking forward to seeing their grandchildren for the first time, uncertain people travelling to new cities for new lives, unaccompanied kids (the airborne balls in a game of Family Law Ping-Pong), sad lovers, happy lovers, expectant mothers, those travelling for life-saving medical treatment, fly-in/fly-out miners and oil rig workers, newly-married honeymoon couples, as well as someone who has saved every week for ten years for this holiday and can quote every word of the fine print in their well-thumbed holiday brochure.

And that catatonic lady over yonder. Never been on a plane before; going to pick up the body of her dead son who was killed on a motorcycle during his gap-year holiday. It seems there is one on every second flight. Now you understand that tact and diplomacy of the cabin crew who seeing "Bereaved Passenger" on the passenger manifest discretely move the middle-aged lady into business class.

    Everyone has got a mother, and mothers aren't meant to outlive their kids.

    It would be interesting to survey a plane load of people and discover their collective Holmes and Rahe Stress Scale[2] ratings.

    The reason for the flight is the main key to a good flight.

    Maybe it would be better to use FedEx for the documents, spend money on video conferencing instead, and save your flight for a relaxing holiday.

2. The Right Airline

You can have a good flight by choosing the right airline.

Marketing departments would have you choose your airline by its color scheme, the advertising music, catering and cabin service "experience", seat pitch, the addition of the business class bar, your own hotel suite in first, or the quality of their movies. Not forgetting a restaurant style menu chosen by a television chef. But what you really want to choose your airline by are its standard operating procedures and the rigor to which those procedures are adhered.

You want spare parts that are purchased directly from the manufacturers, not from a "parts pooling" company where you are more likely to find counterfeit parts. With engineers who, in the middle of the night shift, are going to make the effort to get that tail-stand to double check that the top rudder bearings have been greased because they have pride in their work. With pilots who are tested in the simulators at least twice a year.

Whose trained cabin crew have the latest communications with MedAire's Medlink[3] specialists in Arizona and all the required medical equipment, including a defibrillator, on board all of their flights. Remember, after a heart attack, the chance of recovery without a defibrillator is about 2%. You need one to get you going again.

Whose every sector does not arrive at a hub in the middle of the Inter-Tropical Convergence Zone[4] near the equator; because you want to avoid thunderstorms, not go to where they breed.

These airlines cost money. But in reality the airfare is such a small component of your holiday; what do you care if the best airlines cost an extra $300 or $500? Pay the money, and get a cheaper hotel room. Why do you need such an expensive hotel anyway, you're only there to sleep?

The right airline has a good safety record.

If you are traveling for all the right reasons, and have discarded the concept of flying seven hours for less than the price of your taxi to the airport; now is the time to start planning by getting into the swing of things weeks ahead.

James Nixon

3. Passport

Ensure your passport is valid, and also for each member of your family. Leaving the kids at the airport with the grandparents saying: "I could have sworn the kiddies' passports were up to date" may get you a romantic holiday with your spouse, but remember that your parents know all the tricks to get revenge. They have been around much longer than you.

Returning the children to you after having served chocolate milkshakes laced with laxatives on the morning of your arrival home can make jet lag seem tame by comparison.

Each country has rules before issuing visas. Most require that your passport is valid for six months from the date of entry into the country in question — not the start of your holiday.

James Nixon

    Print e-tickets onto paper and use your passports as ticket holders. The night before you leave, bluetack a large note on the front door:
    Passports / Tickets / Visas?

4. Visas

Ensure there is enough room for the Visas in your passport. Countries whose leaders wear uniforms with tassels on their shoulders and a piece of rope tying their arm to their belt tend to demand a full page to affix their colorful visas. Lots of empty pages are needed for some holidays, and some destinations require your passport a long time before the visa is approved.

A travel writer friend was not allowed onto an Air India flight at Shanghai for his transit in Delhi because he did not have a visa for India. Even though he was doing nothing more than swapping onto a Sri Lankan Airlines flight in the terminal. No way in the world could he convince the Chinese check-in staff that he wouldn't swoon as soon as he saw Delhi from the air and decide to try to enter the country illegally.

('They've obviously never seen the pollution in Delhi,' I told him. *'Everyone knows you can't see it until 200 feet before touchdown.'*)

His job? Traveling as a guest on Air India's new Boeing 787 to write a story about the new airplane. Have a guess how his review went since the plane took off without him?

Never underestimate the number of people who arrive at their departure airport without the correct visas each day. Without them, airline staff would never get seats on staff travel. Triple check your visa.

5. Travel Agent

For that reason alone, you cannot beat the worth of a good travel agent. They are the Visa experts.

A large number of people have stuffed-up their own bookings on the internet. Twice now, people have arrived at the airport in Sydney, Nova Scotia in Canada wondering if they can take a tour of the distinctive bridge and opera house. One guy interviewed on television said that he wondered when he boarded the Sixteen Seater at Halifax;

'I thought Australia was more popular than this.'

And thousands have realized, at the last second, *today* is our return flight. That bloody International Date Line gets you every time …

When you book with a travel agent, they cannot book you on flights which are inside the International Air Transport Association[5](IATA) transit connection limit. So you and your baggage will connect. They arrange your itinerary, check your passport and arrange the visas. They have access to special discounts and hotel package deals and cost you nothing. Travel agents survive on commission from the airlines.

But the best thing is that you can call them from check-in at an airport and ask them to arrange something. Within minutes you are relaxing in your seat and they are emailing confirmations, since your credit card is on their record. On some carriers, your updated e-tickets come straight to your phone in-flight.

James Bond couldn't function without Miss Moneypenny. You can't function without a travel agent. Get a good one, and you'll keep them for life.

While you are planning your flights, think about airport transit hotels. Singapore has a great one, including a rooftop swimming pool. You can be in your room within ten minutes of exiting your plane, sleep restfully in the spartan but adequate room, then spend time by the pool on the roof before your next flight. Capped-off by a foot massage, it can make breaking the trip worthwhile if, by using multiple carriers, you make substantial savings. Your travel agent can arrange the transit hotel bookings at the same time as you buy the tickets. Most big airports have them, but there are only a small number of rooms, so book early.

From The Logbook

Why I love Travel Agents #1

My Bristol travel agent booked me on the Eurostar from London to Paris. A special deal gave me a hotel room for 95 euros a night. Deciding to stay an extra night I went downstairs and tried to extend.

'Mon Plaisir!' the happy receptionist beamed, *'... for an extra 390 Euros.'*

The 95 euro deal was most certainly only for travel agents.

I emailed my travel agent and within five minutes he faxed the hotel, (who still uses fax?). The receptionist then extended me for 95 euros.

Why I love Travel Agents #2

At check-in after a twelve-hour transit at Hong Kong, a Cathay check-in lady demanded to charge excess baggage, (she was obviously trying to raise money to buy a new aircraft).

I called my Bahraini travel agent and asked him to clarify my ticket conditions to the Cathay lady, then handed her the phone. I have no idea what he said but she smiled, apologized and processed my ticket, no extra charge.

6. Earplugs & Eye Shades

They don't call New York the city that never sleeps for nothing. At 3 a.m. on Sunday mornings, it's normal for taxi drivers to honk their horns at pedestrians crossing legally with total disregard for those trying to sleep above. And you have not lived until you have heard the never-ending thrum of Vietnamese motorcycles outside your room, or the sunrise rooster during your idyllic Pacific Island holiday. If you dare to stay up late every night on some islands you will end your holiday seriously sleep-deprived.

Train yourself to use earplugs and eye shades, they can make it easier to sleep on your flights and at your destination. It takes about two weeks to get used to sleeping with ear plugs and eye shades, so start tonight.

Ear Plugs

Obtain some earplugs with the maximum Noise Reduction Rating (NRR) of 32 decibels, the industrial strength foam plugs available from pharmacies.

There is a correct way to insert them, compressing and rolling them, using your saliva to make a perfect seal, then insert and hold them in position for ten seconds until the foam expands. You need to gain confidence that you can still hear Cabin Crew's Emergency PAs and alarm clocks whilst the ear plugs are masking nearly all of the extraneous noise.

Eventually, you will become proficient at sleeping while using earplugs and may choose to use them all the time.

Eye Shades

There are various types of sleep mask, often handed out by airlines, but you can't trust that they will be available on your flight since they only hand them out on night flights.

Online seller Hibermate.com[6], make very comfortable silk sleep masks, some models incorporate ear muffs as well.

James Nixon

7. Frequent Flier

Go online and join the airline's frequent flier program today. Even if you make a temporary card made of paper, joining ensures that you start accruing points from the first sector. You may also be entitled to check-in privileges, airport lounges, and upgrades. All you need is a membership number for the check-in computer.

Since the introduction of K-Class (computerized ticketing) in the 1990s, airlines consistently refine the sales offering to ensure that the planes are full. Starting two years out, when they open flights, passenger loadings are examined at various points on the time scale to see how the flight is filling. Fares are tweaked and promotions are added to attract the right numbers at the "gates" when the passenger loads are examined (18 months out, 1 year, six months and so on).

Empty airline seats are worth nothing as soon as the door is closed, and the industry is distinctive in that, unless they bought tickets together, no passenger knows what the person sitting next to them has paid. Imagine opening a bakery on that premise? It's magic. It allows them to defeat the fickle nature of the general public who also cover themselves by double-booking on multiple flights, even other airlines, to make sure they can travel whenever it suits them.

People traveling for business are happy to pay extra for fully flexible tickets, in case their meeting runs over or the client wants to go for a drink or dinner after the deal is done. Which means that the airline has no idea how many people are going to turn up on the day. Using historical data, (this flight's loads will change based on day of the week if nothing else) they overbook Economy, on some flights up to 120%.

The passengers with money who the airline wishes to look after most of all are not always those traveling in First class or Business, whose tickets are paid by their company or government. It's the small-business travelers in the first few rows of Economy. Unlike the corporates who demand, and get, about 50% discount for bulk-buying; the small business owner must have full flexibility and is paying full retail.

Overbooking Economy allows the flight to go as full as possible. The airline knows that some people are going to miss their flight, others discover at check-in that they don't satisfy the ultimate destination's visa requirements, or that their passport is about to expire, or they have left it at home. Others arrived so early that the airline offered to put them on an earlier flight.

The check-in process continues and people who matter to the airline's future, frequent fliers, are given upgrades into the next class of travel. By exposing them to the higher class it is hoped that next time, they will buy the more expensive ticket. Business up into First, and Economy into Business. Then, when the counters close only forty-five minutes to the flight, staff travel seats are used to fill up the plane if there is anything left. The golden days of airline staff travel are over.

That is why you join the Frequent Flyer program. You are hoping that they have overbooked and you are there to help them out of a spot. But you have to look the part. If they have to upgrade someone and there are two options, the well-dressed person wins every time.

Which is why I have this motto: "There are only two places that miracles happen on a daily basis: Hospital Emergency Rooms and Airport Check-In Counters." I am the only person who wears a smart suit every time I go on holiday, and I go out of my way to help the airline by being ready to assume a higher grade seat if they need.

8. Credit Cards & Lounges

Read the fine print that comes with your credit card. In many cases, if you bought your air ticket with it, you are entitled to free travel insurance. Their website will have the latest details.

Often credit cards entitle you to access airport lounges, say, five times a year. You can often put up with Economy on multiple sector trips, provided that you have access to the oasis that is an airport lounge during a stopover.

If you cannot get free lounge access with your ticket or credit card, check out the lounges at your planned airports by looking at each airport's website. You can also join lounge clubs and receive special treatment,

(PriorityPass[7], Lounge Pass[8], and Lounge Club[9]).

    Large airports have lounge access where you pay on the day, but for some reason, they try to keep it a secret on their websites. Get your eight-year-old niece to search your intended airports. She'll find it in seconds. Or look at The Guide To Sleeping In Airports[10] website.

9. Travel insurance

If you don't think travel insurance can help you relax on your flight, try having a ski holiday in the U.S.A. without it. Unplanned medical bills can ruin your life, even if the injury is minor.

After a motorbike crash, you would hate having to remain behind in a third-world hospital whilst your fellow survivor is airlifted by medivac to Singapore for first-class treatment, because they had better insurance than you.

Choosing travel insurance can be like crossing a legal minefield blindfolded. It takes time to weigh-up the offerings, and thankfully there are comparison websites for each country. Important factors that may concern you are:

- Your age,
- Your gender,
- Your pre-existing illnesses and medications,
- Any illegal or "dangerous" sports or activities you may undertake,
- Baggage allowances, and
- Items that may have to be listed, or even insured, separately.

Nearly all travel insurers offer 24-hour on-call services, some may require you to call for approval before incurring costs during your trip. It's all in the fine print.

Most only sell 60-day policies. What if you want to extend, or worse, what happens if you have an injury that prevents you traveling home before the policy expires?

Make no mistake, travel insurance is a necessity, but each policy has what lawyers call "the hand grenade clause" — one paragraph that they can use to avoid paying-out at all if you haven't complied with every aspect.

One ex-lawyer remarked:

"Never lie to them. Disclose everything at the start, no matter how ridiculous it may seem. A failure to disclose could result in a failure to get a payment."

Airlines can let you down, and their fine print covers them. They have no legal requirement to help you after leaving you stranded without your bags in a foreign port, only a moral one. Not worth the paper it isn't written on. In such a case, it is your travel insurer who will be reimbursing you for the hotel room and extortionate air fares to get you home, so choose wisely.

James Nixon

10. Meals, Seats & Online Check-In

Investigate the seating and meal options no later than a week before the flight. For some airlines, the "special meal" order cutoff may be two weeks out.

SeatGuru.com[11] has configurations for all main airlines including reviews of the best and worst places to sit. Study your flight, know which type of aircraft you'll be catching and choose your seat. An aisle seat is preferable if you intend to roam the airplane. Excellent for a quick getaway, you can leave your finished meal tray in place and slide out.

Get friendly with your airline's frequent flier website. Fill in as much of your profile as you can. If your bladder can stand it, choose a window seat, midway from the noisy toilets and galley, as far away from the cabin bulkheads which will be the location of the on-board bassinets.

Since the special meals get served first, always book a special meal. The low fat or vegetarian options are acceptable. Your mission is to be served straight away, then use the bathroom first; retiring to watch a pre-sleep movie before your fellow passengers finish eating. The state of the washrooms is going to deteriorate. (Unless you fly the airline with the showers in First Class. Their A380s have two diligent cabin service attendants who clean all the washrooms every half an hour.)

Two days before you fly, set alarms to make sure you are ready to click as soon as online check-in opens, and grab your seat. Be aware that some flights actually commence in another city or country and your port is the stopover. If so, many seats will have gone already. Have a backup plan since you will start seeing seats fill-up as soon as the flight opens.

11. Audiobooks

Join Audible.com[12] and buy twelve credits for whatever they charge, (it'll bring the price down to about $10 each). Then choose about six audio books of varying tastes:

- Thrillers
- Romance
- Detective stories
- Self-help books
- Biographies and other non-fiction

Download the books to a phone app or iPod and you are set to tackle even the most daunting delays. Every airport sells Sennheiser ear buds[13] which make listening a pleasure.

Huge headphones are heavy, hot and expensive, and are not necessary for audiobooks.

You will be surprised how enjoyable waiting in lines or departure lounges can become. Having already started a lengthy book before the flight will make it easier. Good luck trying to remember all the characters' names in the first hour of an Agatha Christie novel while negotiating an international airport.

The best aspect of audiobook listening in flight, with your eyes shielded by a sleep mask, is that you may drift off to sleep. No problem. When you wake, just rewind to a chapter you remember and start again.

23 Tips To Survive A Long Flight

From the Logbook

New to audiobooks? *"The Millenium Trilogy"* starting with *"The Girl With The Dragon Tattoo"* is a great way to begin, narrated by Simon Vance.

As you will soon find, the narrator can make or break the experience and Audible allows you to listen to a few minutes of each book before you buy. These are all award winners for good reasons, so starting with them may be a good idea.

Males:
America's **Scott Brick** *(661 titles)*, the U.K's **Simon Vance** *(640 titles)* and Australian **Humphrey Bower** *(78 titles)*.

Females:
America's **Katherine Kellgren** *(176 titles)* **January LeVoy** *(70 titles)* and **Lorelei King** *(145 titles)* and Britain's **Fiona Hardingham** *(70 titles)* and **Finty Williams** *(32 titles)*.

James Nixon

12. Change the Channel

Sleep better before your flight by not watching episodes of Air Crash Investigation in the lead-up to your trip. As they are repeated every few months, you will be able to catch-up when you get back home. Anyway, the reason for the crash on the episode you'll miss was fixed in 1983 and is unlikely to reoccur. The reason for *your* crash hasn't been discovered yet!

As you will discover in a later chapter, arriving for your flight after successive sleepless nights is not the way to embark on your long haul flight. Now is not the time to be studying plane crashes.

James Nixon

13. Jet Lag

In a discussion about jet lag, we have to weed out the word *jet*. Talk descends into a discussion of how to have a more comfortable flight *in* the jet which is an important, but separate, issue that we are dealing-with in the other chapters.

Jet lag has to do with the sun, the planet and your position on it. And how fast you get from one place to the other. It's a coincidence that the jet engine has made it possible to be a problem for people other than Russians.

Russians? Well, in history, no other country spans so many time zones. Trying to trick time they have moved from sixteen time zones to eleven 'real' zones. In an effort to make life easier they now have permanent daylight saving which is now their standard time.

Jet lag was a problem for the huge country, close to the Arctic Circle, in that you could buy a ticket on the Trans-Siberian Express from Moscow to Vladivostok and start heading east at 100 kph (62mph), then keep going for one hundred and forty-three hours and twenty minutes. In every other country, an ocean would have got in the way.

You'd have to adjust to it being seven hours earlier when you got out of the train. Your body would still think it was midnight but the sun would be coming up, which is made even creepier to the passengers because all railways in Russia run on Moscow time.

In the same way, all pilots fly on one time zone: Greenwich Mean Time (which became Co-Ordinated Universal Time in 1961 then, to appease the French six years later: Universal Time Co-Ordinated), or UTC. It's only passengers and airports that run on local time. Which is why you sometimes hear pilots giving a public address, letting the passengers know that they are arriving more than an hour early or late. Then instilling a terrifying confidence by adding:

Um, er, that can't be right...'

Leading half the passengers to wonder:

'Oh My God! If he can't even tell the time, how the hell is he gonna land the plane?'

Jet lag is a circadian rhythm problem for humans who are affected by the way the sun shines relative to their established body clock. It's a lesser issue for some blind people, notably the late Ray Charles who stressed-out promotors by refusing to arrive in the city until near the time of his concerts, citing:

'Blind people don't get jet lag. Why do you want me to sit in a hotel room for an extra day?'

Most blind people are affected by jet lag, but to a lesser degree than sighted people. With lives also regulated by the sun, animals must also be affected by jet lag. There is some evidence that race horses can gallop for up to twenty-four seconds longer before fatigue sets in after a long flight. Whether that has to do with jet lag or the exhilaration of not being cooped-up in a plane can never be known.

We get jet lag by crossing time zones in jets. If teleportation, favored by science fiction writers, had taken-off before jets then it'd be called 'teleport lag' if you quickly crossed time zones.

So what's a time zone?

Imagine planet earth. Now put yourself at the top at the True North Pole, where the imaginary pole exists around the axis of rotation. You could stand right on the top. Every direction would be south and you could walk around in circles crossing every time zone in seconds.

Well, you could if it was on land. But it's in the middle of the Arctic Ocean where the sea is 4,261 meters (13,980 feet) deep. The nearest land, an island off Greenland, is about 700 kilometers (435 miles) away. Sure, there's shifting pack-ice but it's easier to perform this trick at the South Pole where the Americans have a base and every direction you look, with your back to the pole, is north.

After "running around the world" you could go inside for a cup of hot chocolate, a clever idea considering the winter low is -60 Celsius (about -76 Fahrenheit) for six months of the year. Compared to only -57 Celsius (-71 Fahrenheit) where airliners cruise.

Grab an orange. For argument's sake, it is now planet earth. Looking down on it you would be confronted with a basic circle, widest at its 'equator.' You could draw a line around the equator. Circles are distinctive because they are divided up into 360 degrees. If we wanted we could put 360 evenly-spaced marks around the equator.

We know that the earth rotates completely every twenty-four hours, counter-clockwise if you are looking down on it. 360 degrees divided by twenty-four hours equals fifteen degrees. Therefore, at the equator, if you went east for fifteen degrees and stopped, you would notice that the sun rose and set an hour earlier, and so on, all the way around.

For fun, on your orange, you could count off these fifteen-degree marks and draw a line from one pole to the other, crossing the marks. In the end, you would have twenty-four segments, fattest at the equator and each converging to a point at each pole.

[Right now, for research purposes, you are considering getting a Terry's Chocolate

Orange ball to prove it. I just did. But instead of 24, there are only 20 segments … no, make that nineteen. *Very tasty.*]

Each one of the LONG lines is called a line of LONGitude. And each one is, for time zone purposes, one hour ahead of (or behind) the one beside it. You can appreciate that running up and down one of the lines will not change your time, relative to when the sun comes up. That's going from the top (north) to the bottom (south) and as long as you stay on your segment, your time doesn't change.

Even if you fly for fourteen hours from Moscow to Johannesburg, despite changing from summer to winter or vice versa, your time, relative to sunrise, doesn't change. No jet lag. You still are going to feel like you have been run over by a truck, but hopefully, that can be lessened by reading the other chapters.

It is only when you go from east to west (sideways) that you start crossing the time zones, playing tricks on your body, and affecting your sleep.

How long it takes to cross those time zones depends on your LATITUDE. For some obscure reason, I remember latitude as

FATitude because the planet is fatter than it is high, by 42.72 kilometers (26.54 miles).

At the equator, the earth is rotating at 1,674 kph (1,040 mph). At Kennedy Space Centre, 31% of the way to the North Pole, it's still doing 1,470 kph (913 mph) which is a significant free ride when you're shooting rockets into space.

The further you go towards the poles, the slower the rotation. At the South Pole you could go and stand a hundred meters away and it would take twenty-four hours to get back to the same spot. [Forgetting the fact that earth would be 2,592,000 km (1,610,591 miles) further along its annual trip around the sun.]

Latitude is also divided into degrees, with the Equator being 0 and the poles being 90 degrees north and south.

Eighty degrees north or south of the equator (only ten degrees from the poles) is still too cold for humans, being only 1,111 km (690 miles) away, but at this distance the earth's rotational speed is noticeable at about 290 kph (180 mph).

About sixty degrees north, where we find Québec, St. Petersburg and Scotland's

Shetland Islands you are heading eastward at a lazy 835kph (518 mph) which makes for relaxing sunrises and sunsets, unlike the "lights on, lights off" shock that greets first timers holidaying near the equator. *You have to be quick if you want to share a romantic sunset in Singapore.*

The width of a time zone segment at the equator is 1,670 km (1,037 miles), and half that at St. Petersburg. Another reason why it's easy to cross so many zones in Russia. At those latitudes the distances are manageable.

As you cross more time zones, the more your body is going to be confused when you stop. And while you can get used to the changes through education and experience, you can't stop getting jet lag. It is a badge of honor, proving that you have indeed, circumnavigated the planet. It's only proper that you feel different. Millions before you died trying to do what you just did.

The effects are worse heading east, as you "lose" time. Seven hours' time difference from the Middle East to Australia's east coast and you are ready for bed when everyone, the sun included, is waking-up. Your body feels cheated and misses out on sleep.

Heading west, say from the Middle East to New York, your day goes on forever. You 'make' time. After twelve hours of traveling it's still mid-afternoon. You hit the hotel room and, as the sun goes down, you happily fall asleep.

The effects of jet lag vary, but they break down into three groups:

- Physiological
- Mental
- Sleep

Physiological

Your body behaves as it would in the old time zone when you are in another. It takes a day to catch up one or two time zones. A London to Sydney trip will take about five to six days to adjust. As well as constipation and/or diarrhea, first-timers at long-haul travel never fail to notice that their bowel movements now occur at different times of the day. For someone who has always had a morning bowel movement, it can be disconcerting that this now occurs in mid-afternoon, or last thing at night.

One high-flying VVIP business mogul tries to beat this by having nothing in his bowel during a flight. He is so convinced that a clean bowel is a key to beating jet lag that he has a colonic irrigation session prior to each long-haul flight in his corporate jet. He is in his 80s, so who's to say it doesn't work?

The Mayo Clinic website provides healthy skepticism by suggesting that the human body, well nourished, is perfectly good at ridding itself of waste. And has been for centuries. A lubricated firehose, no matter how well-meaning, should not be introduced into the area.

Irritability, nausea, sweating, dehydration, and headaches are not caused by jet lag but by the mode of transport. As are the muscle cramps, and menstrual problems.
If you could transit the same number of time zones without the:

- Departure airport experience
- Stress of leaving

- Rapid temperature changes
- Claustrophobic experience
- Mild hypoxia
- Mild deep vein thrombosis
- Arrival airport experience,

then most symptoms attributed to jet lag would be eliminated. And can be for the seasoned traveler.

Mental

The mental fuzziness, confusion, and problems trying to concentrate on the simplest of tasks seem to be jet lag related. No matter how well you travel, chances are that you find yourself making silly mistakes upon arrival.

With that in mind, do not hire a car at Los Angeles airport after a fifteen-hour flight and plan to do battle with the peak hour traffic if you have never driven on the right-hand side of the road before. Hire car companies report that most of their customer crashes occur within twenty minutes of the LAX car parks.

Be wary about signing important deals or contracts when you are expecting to be jet lagged. Go over the contract details before you leave instead and, if necessary, walk straight into a meeting from the plane. But be wary of the dreaded third day.

For large time zone changes the third day is when your body gives up trying to play the game. When you least expect it an overwhelming tiredness hits you. Give in and sleep as long as you need. Plan for it by clearing your diary in advance. Pushing through, using caffeine and will-power, is an option. Apologize to your family, friends and work colleagues in advance. You will be crabby.

Sadly for aircrew, the third day often coincides with their next trip. Luckily for them, since they were only in the other time zone for a brief stay, their jet lag is not as pronounced as the relocating expat passenger, business traveler, or holidaymaker.

Often they will stay in their home time zone, which is quite acceptable with 24-hour room service. It astounds even the most seasoned aircrew when arriving in USA hotels that room service is usually closed from midnight to six in the morning. They do, however, always have access to an extremely noisy ice machine. How do I know? *It was always next to my room.*

Sleep

Often the first time a person experiences insomnia is when suffering from jet lag. Being dog-tired yet unable to sleep, rolling around in a hotel bed knowing that your arm has NEVER been in this position before in your whole life. *("How did I ever sleep with THIS hanging off my neck?")*

Other times you crash so hard before you undress, or turn off the television or lights, waking with a cricked-neck, pounding headache, and that bloody Sky News theme blaring from the TV. Or you're like a petulant three-year-old, snapping at family members, and then falling asleep at the dining table. Worse, you know that you are behaving badly, and can't help yourself.

On day three, don't make appointments or important plans. Be ready to give in, whatever time it hits you. If it's a mid-afternoon nap that lasts eight or ten hours, so be it.

Jet lag cures

Nothing can be taken to speed-up the joining of your body with your new location on the planet except for time, water and sunshine. Take as much of each as you need. A cup of tea and a sit in the sun, with a cat or puppy on your lap, is all you need.

The general rule is that you should stay up until local bedtime, which may be difficult if you have been flying all night and landed at dawn. In that case, grab a few hours' sleep and force yourself to wake after a few hours, then push through until dark.

Get onto your new time zone, psychologically, as soon as you can. Up to a week ahead, start bringing your sleep earlier if you are headed east. Listen to destination radio stations on TuneIn Radio and be aware of their local time. Read their newspapers online and start following the local issues. Put your watch on destination time at the start of the flight.

Understand that no pills, or magical cures can hasten recovery. There is an entire industry trying to convince you otherwise. They are wrong, and are all trying to rip you off. Be kind to yourself and your wallet. If you are aircrew embarking on a long haul career, or have a new job that entails regular business travel, understand that while you can learn to manage it, or rather, your personal reactions to shifting time zones, you can't *beat* it.

So stop trying.

From the Logbook

I come from the land down under, where we drive on the left side of the road. When I am in countries that drive on the left I only drive manual cars. When I am countries that drive on the right, I only drive automatic cars, realizing that when I have an emergency behind the wheel I will not have the years of subconscious experience to help me. Knowing this, I limit the amount of brain capacity needed to drive when jet-lagged.

***

James Nixon

Our first A380 flights to New York saw us arriving about 2 p.m. local which, to our bodies, was 11 p.m. No matter what we did, we were asleep on our feet by 9 p.m. local. At 4 a.m. New York time we were wide awake, when the only thing open was the diner behind the hotel, and the Apple store. Drinking their coffee at the diner, cops would sit watching the only life visible on the streets: a steady stream of wide-eyed aircrew coming back from the Apple store with the distinctive white shopping bags.

***

When we first started flying the A380 from the Middle East, our only destinations were the U.S.A., and Australia. For two years our body clocks were between Bali and Singapore or between Iceland and Greenland. Never in the same place as our bodies. Hundreds of pilots and cabin crew missed birthdays, medical and dental appointments, dinner parties, lunch catchups and everything in between.

Were we sleeping?

Nope, just lying on the couch staring at *Air Crash Investigations, Mega Machines* and *MythBusters*. Too trashed to change channels, even though the remotes were in our hands.

Jet lag is like that.

***

I am thinking of starting a kitten and puppy rental service for jet-lagged aircrew. You get back from a trip, and dial 888, *Paws&Tea Jet lag Rescue*.

A vehicle resembling an ambulance speeds through the city and comes to your house. Doors open and two uniformed experts set you up with a comfortable deck chair in the sunshine. One puts a puppy in your lap while the other makes you a cup of tea.

Then they are off to respond to other calls. After an hour or so they return to rescue the poor animal and replace it with a fresh one. They might even care enough to make you another cup of tea.

***

Jen and Jim are a retired Australian couple who were on last leg of their "world tour of churches" (or so it seemed to Jim).

They arrived in America, where people drive on the wrong side of the road. Severely jet-lagged, and a nearing the limit of his politeness, Jim drove out of the rental car park immediately onto the majestic American highway system. For first timers it is awe-inspiring. Within seconds you forget about where you are meant to be going, swept along in a tsunami of cars.

Eventually spying his exit he made it onto the off-ramp that soon became one of those freeway cloverleaf affairs that Australians had only seen on Bugs Bunny cartoons. He and Jen weren't on speaking terms at that stage, when his hand brushed the steering wheel indicator stalk.

The previous hirer of the car must have been running late to get to the airport and had set the cruise-control to warp speed. It now re-engaged.

Never having used cruise-control in his life, Jim had no idea why, entering a 270 degree turn, his car should decide to automatically accelerate to the speed of sound. Steering suddenly occupied all his attention.

As sweat instantly broke out from every pore, Jen was sitting, arms crossed in the passenger seat thinking: *'You can't scare me!'* About halfway around the turn he found the brake pedal, which disconnected the cruise control.

You can still drive a car with jet lag, but have little spare capacity for anything else.

... Amazingly, they are still married.

James Nixon

14. Deal With The Fear

Recognize (talking to non-Pilots here, I hope) if you have a slight fear of flying. This can affect your sleep patterns leading up to the flight, and throughout your entire career as a passenger. In the weeks before you take off you can work on these fears by getting educated about the "Principles of Flight[14]." You will be in the minority of passengers on your flight who understands why you leave the earth.

Understanding that you are, more than likely, a person who likes to be in control — I didn't say control-freak — makes it easy to see why flying is an issue. It's this relinquishing of control to unseen people that makes flying difficult.

Further research on the quality of training of the flight crews, and the highly-supervised work of the engineers and air traffic controllers should also give you confidence.

Before 9/11, we used to have passengers sit in the jump seats behind the pilots to share the view of take-off and landing. The most fearful flyer was instantly cured as they felt part of the crew with their headset on, listening to Air Traffic Control, and being able to see out the front. More than a few went on to become private pilots themselves.

Some airlines have magical in-flight video cameras, "pilot eye view" and even "tail cam" on the A380. Make sure you work out these controls as soon as you sit in your seat for the full wide-screen view (see if you can catch the tug driver sending SMS messages to his wife while waiting for the baggage loading to finish).

YouTube has some fantastic in-cockpit footage of take-off and landings. Check out the video 'FLYING TIARE - French Polynesia with a go pro - Air Tahiti Nui[15]' celebrating the 15th birthday of the Air Tahiti's Airbus A340. It is captivating. Knowing what is happening up front makes it easier to relax.

If you have a chronic fear of flying, check with your airline well in advance. Many run Fear of Flying courses for their prospective passengers.

James Nixon

15. Socks

Buy some flight socks, the type that goes to your knee and compresses the lower leg and feet. They are designed to prevent Deep Vein Thrombosis. Having used them on long flights for a decade; I can attest that you will arrive feeling *fresher*.

If nothing else, the compression socks stop your feet swelling, making it easier to get your shoes back on as you reach the destination. Less-bendy people find slip-on shoes helpful for air travel.

A pair of thick oversized hiking socks will also keep your feet warm while you sleep.

James Nixon

16. Plan Ahead

Much pre-flight sleep is lost by worrying about communication. Mobile phone coverage, roaming rates, internet access for email, and ensuring snail-mail is dealt-with back home.

Before you travel, join WhatsApp[16], the world's largest phone system. As long as you have Wi-Fi access, you can send and received texts for free. Not only texts but sound bites and pictures, even free calls in some countries. Check with your overseas friends to see if they also have WhatsApp. You may have to add a second version of their number, complete with country code, before the system finds them in your phone and loads them into the app.

Check with your phone provider. To save you incurring huge bills if your phone is stolen, some companies do not allow global roaming unless you advise them in writing beforehand. And without Wi-Fi at hand, you may need to make calls the minute you land.

Oh, and turn off data-roaming unless you are rich. Come to think of it, data-roaming can make rich people go broke. Leave it off. There's enough free Wi-Fi in the world for you. Or buy a local sim card for longer stays.

It's the same with credit cards. Start using your credit card in a foreign country, especially for small amounts (the way criminals check if the card works), and if you don't answer your bank's call to your home mobile within seconds you can be assured your card will be turned off. Some banks don't even ring. This is not the way to ensure relaxing sleep on the first night of your month-long vacation.

As well as your phone company, contact your credit card help desk and advise them when and where you are traveling. It may be mandatory if you are expecting to use their travel insurance.

17. Doctor

It's hard to sleep in jail (so I am told); well, for the first few nights anyway. You could be headed for a long holiday in a small room if you take controlled drugs across a border. Quite a few countries have restrictions on medications that are widely available in other states. Codeine, cold tablets, antidepressants, sleeping pills and others could land you in hot water.

Ensure your doctor writes a letter detailing your prescriptions and medications, and you will sleep better. You may also need to update your vaccinations. Some countries need to see a vaccination booklet.

And make sure to have two sets of your prescription drugs, one you carry in your hand luggage and the other in your checked baggage.

Your Doctor may need to write a letter to your Travel Insurer, so do all of this way in advance of the flight.

18. Hypoxia & Nicotine

If you are elderly, have a history of lung issues or are a heavy smoker, the alveoli in your lungs –the small sacs that transfer the oxygen into your blood– think you are already at about 8,000 feet above sea level. That is higher than where you would be sleeping at nearly all ski resorts.

Then when you fly, you add the cabin altitude and discover that your lungs think you are already above 15,000 feet. This puts you in the range for mild hypoxia; the name of the condition when you have a lower-than-normal concentration of blood in your arterial blood. By law, you need supplemental oxygen above 14,000 feet, but of course, you are blissfully unaware.

Every person's reaction to hypoxia is different, and with you for life. Some people feel extremely happy, like they had three Mai-Tais on an empty stomach. Other people may become anxious or confused, short of breath, start coughing or wheezing, have a rapid heart rate, even a change in skin color. Some people become argumentative.

We have heard stories of people who have tried to open the aircraft doors at altitude, or demanded to see the captain. Some wanted to fight.

Pilots undertake "chamber runs" in aviation decompression chambers. They are instantly taken from sea level to 25,000 feet in a simulation of an explosive decompression to see their personal effects of hypoxia. There they are observed by a partner who is wearing an oxygen mask while they perform simple tasks: identifying playing cards, writing their name, doing simple math problems, drawing five-pointed stars and finishing by signing their name.

Within seconds their performance is amusing to their partner and other observers. After a minute or two, they are told to put on their own oxygen mask. Most cannot. Their partner, sitting opposite, reaches over and affixes their mask and hits the 100% button. Immediately the victim's color returns and within seconds their faculties have resumed. Having discovered their own symptoms they know that if they ever feel that way again in an airplane, they have to dive for an oxygen mask to remain conscious.

Then the exercise is repeated for their partner and they assume the role of safety pilot. Mind-blowing, considering that minutes earlier they were effectively crippled. The recovery is total. Provided they get oxygen fast enough. YouTube has some impressive videos of hypoxia demonstrations[17].

When a mild to heavy smoker is hypoxic, whose individual symptoms are "being belligerent," and hasn't had a cigarette for three hours, well, let us just say, now you know why people smoke in aircraft toilets and pick fights with crew members. And when you hear that six other passengers piled on top of someone who tried to open a door in flight, you are getting the message.

Why don't airlines offer all passengers who are smokers free nicotine patches, or nicotine chewing gum, so they don't have to suffer withdrawals when we know that they are mildly hypoxic to start with? Wouldn't that be the ultimate in customer service? The answer is "because of the lawyers." Nicotine is a drug and airline staff cannot dish out drugs to passengers. Maybe one-day Medlink doctors will, over the satellite phone, authorize crew to administer nicotine chewing gum, but it's doubtful.

If you have lung issues, you can have supplemental oxygen provided from an oxygen generator. If you are a smoker, get a prescription from your doctor if needed, but don't get on that plane without nicotine patches or nicotine chewing gum to stop you climbing the walls. You will have a better flight.

And the crew won't have to restrain you.

19. Pack Cleverly

Even if you are going away for ten years, they do have shops overseas. Travel as light as you can. Choose outfits that can mix and match. Aim for lightweight clothes and put on a number of layers. Unless you are a full-fledged mountaineer, leave the backpack at home. Grab a daypack and then put it inside an expensive, lightweight, hard shell (bed bug resistant) suitcase that has good wheels and a name that starts with *Samson* and ends with *ite*; or, (according to my Editor) ends in *Tourister*.

Expect that your check-in luggage will go missing. Expect that your carry-on hand baggage will go missing.

In the old days, it was wise to photocopy your passport, visas, credit cards, I.D. cards, (front and back) and hide them in the lining of your luggage and in your carry-on. Even a few Traveler's Checks (remember them, Mr. Wong?) You'd be grateful of them if you got mugged. I still hide a few hundred U.S. dollars emergency money in the lining of my case. If nothing else, it makes a pleasant surprise five years later when you go away again. It can guarantee a Christmas card if you give your old suitcase to your niece.

These days, an internet 'cloud' service like Evernote.com[18] or DropBox.com[19] is invaluable. Scans of every e-ticket, train, hotel and car rental booking, travel insurance details, doctor's letters, prescriptions, as well as all your cards and identity cards can leave your home computer, fly to the cloud, and simultaneously be available on your phone and iPad or from any computer in the world that you can use to log into their site. Make sure that for your trip, your phone and iPad are security locked, and enable the "Find My Phone" option on all your devices.

23 Tips To Survive A Long Flight

The trick to packing quickly is to have a shower. As you dress, for each item you put-on, add multiple numbers of the same item onto your bed. Underwear, pants, shirts, and so-on. When you have finished, cull the number as much as you can.

Youtube has some interesting videos[20] on the art; rolling socks and stuffing them in shoes, layering shirts and so on. Be wary of the videos that interlock all your clothes; that method is great if you are moving house, but you may have to live out of the suitcase for some time.

Packing early and having all your documents secure can help you sleep well on the night before your trip. Few people get a good night's sleep before a flight, so are starting off at a disadvantage.

When you consider how many cranky, sleep-deprived people they have to deal with every day, it makes you respect the check-in staff; who are always grateful if you give them a packet of candies to share after the rush dies down.

James Nixon

20. Get There Early

Say goodbye to your family and friends, defeat traffic and transportation snarls and head to the airport very early. This also counts for Staff Travel. Get to the place where miracles happen early. Even though the upgrades are not handed out until the last thirty minutes —usually at the boarding gate— the check-in staff will appreciate that you came out early to make their lives easier, will have had a chance to see that you are well-dressed, and may even make a mental note to bump you into a higher grade.

You will never get a seat on an overbooked airplane by sitting in a hotel room. Go to the airport, look fantastic, and be early.

James Nixon

The sooner your bags are checked-in and you are holding a boarding pass, the sooner you can relax.

21. Enjoy The Airport

Since the 1990s, many airports have been purchased by shopping center owners. No wonder considering that the top ten airports each see more than sixty million passengers a year, about 165,000 people each day. A captive market if ever there was one.

With the added duty-free and fat holiday wallets, they have turned the concourses into shopper's delights using all the psychological tricks to attract buyers. Dubai Duty Free, servicing the seventy million passengers who pass through one of the world's largest international airports, turns over two billion dollars a year.

Treat yourself to the latest technology pocket-sized camera and a pair of in-ear earphones every time you go on holidays. Sunglasses, watches, and books seem to be mandatory purchases. (It has always confused me why they sell luggage after you have gone through security and customs. Does that guy ever make a sale?)

Expect that the air-conditioning in the airport will be a few degrees too hot. It is cheaper to keep it about 25 Celsius (77 Fahrenheit) instead of 18 Celsius (65 Fahrenheit), plus, you will be more stressed and hence, warmer than usual. This is why I suggest layers of loose-fitting clothing.

Depending on the ground air-conditioning, the aircraft may also be too warm until ten minutes after departure when the aircraft air-conditioning has a chance to work effectively. Later during the flight, depending on where you will be sitting, it could get cool.

Wait until you have gone through security before buying a bottle of water or they will confiscate it from you. (Why? There are some explosives that can be made by mixing two clear liquids.) Once through security buy and keep drinking more water. Make sure you have a fresh bottle when you go onboard.

As well as shopping, your focus is walking, walking, and more walking. Same if you have a ninety-minute stopover. Walk, and keep walking until you are required for boarding. Buy some chocolates or barley sugar to "buy-off" your fellow passengers. You are never going to see them again, so while it is important to be polite, you have to manipulate them to allow you to sleep. Be first on, know where you are sitting, and grab your overhead space. Claim your seat and keep an eye on empty seats nearby. As fast as a striking snake you are going to steal another pillow as a lumbar support if possible. Try to do it so fast that no one notices.

Keep standing and moving, then be pleasant to your arriving fellow travelers. As they settle, make small talk with them and the person beside you; especially the person immediately in front of your seat. Offer a chocolate or barley sugar. As soon as they have accepted, they are subconsciously thinking that you are a nice person and there is less chance that you are going to suffer armrest or seat-back warfare. The crew doesn't mind if you offer them a chocolate either. If you are on an aisle seat, explain before you sleep, (more chocolates), that we are all adults, and it is a matter of getting through this flight:

'If I am asleep and you need to get up and go for a walk, don't be precious, just clamber over me, OK?'

Chances are that they won't even wake you.

Buy a book but don't expect to read. Maybe it is mild hypoxia, but despite best intentions, most people struggle to read while airborne. Audiobooks are popular.

Of course, movies help pass the time, but the loud music and sound effects may tend to prevent sleep. If it is about that cute Labrador, "Marley and Me", you can expect that a flight attendant will materialize to ask if you want anything just as you are bursting into tears. Not giving away the ending here, but they stand behind you waiting for the moment. I am sure they do. Mild hypoxia makes grown men cry at the movies.

23 Tips To Survive A Long Flight

Time your arrival at the gate so that you don't need to sit with "the masses." They will give a pre-boarding announcement for people with small kids. Ideally, you walk straight to the front of the line as others are hearing the boarding P.A. You don't want to breathe anyone's cold germs, and airport boarding lounge air-conditioning is no-where near as effective as that on the aircraft.

James Nixon

22. On The Aircraft

Inside the aircraft, the air is admitted above your head and extracted at floor level (it is wise to position the gasper vent so as to provide a constant curtain of air). Theoretically, you can't breathe air from anyone even one row in front or behind you. It passes through filters that are equivalent to (the manufacturer's say better than) the filters used in hospital operating theatres. A percentage flows into the cargo compartment and is exhausted overboard, and the rest is filtered again and mixed with fresh air from the front of the jet engines.

The air in an A380 is changed every three minutes. The pilots can seal up cargo compartments and extract cabin air directly overboard in case of smoke or fumes, with the flick of a switch. All the air in the toilets is, thankfully, extracted overboard.

While being cleaned of 99% of the nasty germs, the air is low in humidity. It is around 12%, which is drier than normal. The only way to defeat the drying-out of your skin is to add moisturizer; and for the mucus in your airways, to add water. Lots of ingested water. If you are feeling thirsty you are already dehydrated.

Contact germs from touching surfaces, and then your face and eyes, can be defeated by a hand sanitizer. Buy the 50ml bottle as 100 ml bottles may be confiscated by airport security. Wipes may be easier.

Move in your seat. Every twenty minutes or so move your feet, toes, and legs to get your blood flowing. Shrug your shoulders, twist and turn your neck. The adage of walking around the airplane is a nice concept, but impractical. Some people do it, and maybe it works for them. If the seatbelt sign is on and you are walking around, and the plane hits clear air turbulence, you can forget being compensated by the airline. If your flying body breaks a child's neck, it could be the most expensive flight of your life.

The aisle-walkers would benefit more by staying in their seats, doing leg exercises, and learning to deep breathe. Hours breathing off the top of your lungs must add to the mild hypoxia. Whenever you think of it, try three huge deep breaths in a row, emptying your lungs, holding it, then filling your lungs to capacity, then a little more, and even more; hold it before repeating.

Sleeping on long flights can be assisted by knowing that your money and documents are secured in your cabin baggage in such a way that a quick thief opening the overhead bins would be foiled and move on to an easier mark. When you wake, you should be able to reach out without lifting your eye mask. Grab your bottle, have a sip of water, then pop a barley sugar or chocolate in your mouth for a sugar hit, and drift back off to sleep.

James Nixon

23. The Approach & Landing

Arrange yourself so that your phone, wallet, and passport are on your person before takeoff, and for the approach and landing —in case you have to do an emergency evacuation.

Look at the emergency exits around you and make a note if you are going to go forward or back. The seats fold forward once their passengers have gone and jammed the aisle. Going forward beside the wall may be an option.

A documentary interviewed survivors from all sorts of disasters: tsunami, shipping disaster, air crash and building fire. Every victim had made a conscious decision that they were not going to die that day and reacted accordingly. When disaster strikes, it strikes hard, and you have to get tough or die.

Have a plan.

Now we have covered the morbid side of landing; don't forget to watch the approach on TV if you can, especially from tail-cam if it is available. The pilot will be looking at the aiming point (the two big white boxes) in the middle of the touchdown zone. There are also some red and white lights next to it.

The touchdown zone is a box that extends to 900 meters (980 yards) down the runway. The large white boxes start 400 meters (440 yards) from the start of the runway. The manufacturer (and you) wants the aircraft to be touching down inside the zone which, incidentally, is longer than the tallest man-made building is high. The runway is three or four kilometers (two to three miles) long, so you have heaps of margin.

As the pilots approach the touchdown zone, it is coming at them at 260 kph (160 mph). They switch their focal point to the end of the runway and start flaring the aircraft. You can see as the image tilts up. At the same time thrust is reduced. The wings squash the air trapped between them and the runway, like balloons, and the plane settles onto the ground.

If the wind is coming from the side, they will crab along the center line then, in the flare, squeeze the rudder (with foot pedals) to point the nose down the runway. With a tiny flick of the wrist they will put the main wheel on the windward side onto the ground first, then the other side, and then the nose.

If the runway is contaminated they will go for a "positive touchdown" to ensure the rubber of the wheels gets through the slush onto the runway.

As soon as the main wheels settle onto the runway, the top of the wings open up. This dumps all the lift and puts the weight onto the wheels –allowing the brakes to work efficiently. They may also select reverse thrust, although it is not needed unless the runways are contaminated.

If you can see the engines you will see the sides open up. The exhaust which had been going out the back will now be directed forward. It's effective at high speed, and these will be stowed by 140 kph (85 mph) so they don't kick up debris which could then get sucked into the front of the engines.

Relax and go with it.

If your great-grandfather could see you now, he would be jealous. Mankind has waited centuries to do what you are doing.

And you're doing it without even messing up your hair.

The Checklist

- Make sure you're flying for the right reasons, if you can.
- Choose a safe airline.
- Make sure passports and visas are correct.
- Use a travel agent.
- Start using earplugs and eye shades.
- Join the frequent flier programs of your intended airlines.
- Check the benefits fine print and notify your credit card's providers.

- See if you can obtain access to airport lounges.
- Choose the right travel insurance.
- Buy audiobooks.
- Stop watching air crash channels.
- Start to time-travel towards your destination to lessen effects of jet lag.
- Deal with the fear.
- Plan ahead: copy documents, contact banks, phone providers.
- Get compression socks.
- See your doctor about your drugs, get a letter if needed.
- If you have lung issues, see your Doctor about using supplemental oxygen.
- If you smoke, get nicotine gum or patches.
- Order special meals through the frequent flyer website

23 Tips To Survive A Long Flight

- Be online the second check-in begins and choose your seats.
- Pack cleverly.
- Get to the airport and go through security early.
- After security, buy hand sanitizer, water, and chocolate bribes.
- Walk, Walk, Walk.
- On board, greet your fellow passengers.
- Make sure they can't steal your goodies.
- Keep valuables close during takeoff and landing.
- Drive extra carefully after you land.
- Clear your diary three days after a long flight and give in to jetlag.
- Enjoy the experience.

James Nixon

What's Next?

If you have enjoyed this short book I would be grateful if you would go to Amazon's kindle page and post an honest review.

An author's life is a solitary one, tapping keys in the silence of the office. Reviews on the Amazon site are the reward for all the work. The more reviews from locations all around the world, the more people will be able to see the book. It's that simple. It's the new word-of-mouth. It's what authors live for.

My dream is to get onto the best-seller lists which can help a book to "breakout" from the masses and gain real attention. Your book review will really help me.

If you would like to recommend it on your social media, that'd be great too. I really value your feedback, please email me at:
james@CrammondMedia.com
Whilst I may not be able to reply personally, I promise to read every message. I will reply by tweets (@crammond) to enable all readers to benefit from our conversation.

Join my reader's list to follow my work & get updates on my next books and, sometimes, free stuff.

http://www.jamesnixon.com/JoinMe/

Acknowledgements

Michael Blamey – Proofreader.

Lynn & Len Hallett
 – great family friends,
 and addicted travelers.

Ian Hunt – Reviewer.

Patrick McMahon – Proofreader.

Navjot Singh – Proofreader.

Chris Sotiropoulos – Legal Counsel.

Kerryn Warner – Personal Assistant.

James Nixon

Other Books by James Nixon

SLEEPING FOR PILOTS & CABIN CREW
(And Other Insomniacs)

by
James Nixon
(The Anonymous Airbus A380 Captain)*

The book that lifts the sheets on how to sleep whenever YOU want.

Getting control of their sleep is the only way new aircrew can turn their job into a long-term career.

Divided into two parts, the first half of this book is an analysis of the 20 variables that can affect your sleep. The second half is the 'how-to' section. Tips and tricks tested in the laboratory of life, the harshest conditions in the world: the moving sleep cycle of the international flight crew.

Like no-one else does it.

James Nixon

Fire fighters, police, doctors, nurses, shift workers all get a roster that allows a sign-on at the same time for up to six days in a row. They feel like crap, but they can get a routine going.

Aircrew rise before the sun, fly to a location, arrive in the late afternoon, have twenty-two hours off then fly back all night — arriving before the sun rises on day three. On day four they sign-on in the afternoon and fly until midnight. And so on. If they are traveling east and west then jet lag adds to the mix.

There are entire industries trying to sell you things to sleep faster, better, easier, softer and longer. Few of them work. Some are outright dangerous and can put flight crew licenses at risk, not to mention the lives of their passengers.

This is the book you would have written if you had interviewed a few thirty-year veterans and spent about a year of your days-off trolling through the published research papers, newspaper and magazine stories, and websites.

James Nixon has tried to distill some heavy topics into light reading; and can guarantee that if the reader does everything he suggests, they will get control of their sleep; sleeping better than they've ever slept before.

To reinforce points, he has included "From The Logbook" sections which give amusing anecdotes. Feedback is that readers love these insights.

The section on Stress Management resulted in the book becoming a Kindle Bestseller.

* When he wrote the book, his employment contract precluded writing under his own name.

Go to the Amazon site for the eBook
& paperback
http://tinyurl.com/SleepingForPilots

Also available at your local bookstore
(They may have to order it in for you)

Australian readers can get the paperback, saving both time and money, from:
www.JamesNixonBooks.com

or visit

www.ProfessionalSleeping.com

James Nixon

Reader Reviews

Essential Reading For Aircrew
(& anyone else working the backside of the clock)

'I gave up a career that I loved, in large part because the night shifts, and subsequent fatigue, were killing me. Had this informative, well researched, and humorous book been available, I might still be flying.'
IH, (former) A380 Captain

***

'Trying to study for the simulator but made the fatal mistake of uploading "Sleeping For Pilots & Cabin Crew" onto my kindle!

I cannot put it down and am laughing out loud at some anecdotes.

Every shift worker needs this book! ... as entertaining as Bill Bryson's books I reckon! '

CJ, Boeing 777 Captain

James Nixon

Highly Recommended

'Not only will this book benefit Pilots, Cabin Crew, and other insomniacs, but I consider this to be a great companion book for any traveler.

A delightful and easy read, with well-researched topics full of great information and very useful tips ... from the effects of low Vitamin D levels, Mosquitoes, and the prevention/precautions of Malaria and other related diseases, prescription, over the counter meds and illegal drugs are just a few of the many topics which I found particularly interesting.

Oh, and the thought of Bed Bugs will no doubt be lingering in the back of my mind when next I check into a hotel room.

But what I enjoyed reading the most was the Author's Logbook stories which were so wonderfully entertaining. So, if he were to consider a future book compiling stories from his travels over the last few decades, I'd snap it up in a heartbeat!'

NL, (ex Flight Attendant)

23 Tips To Survive A Long Flight

***

Read the 36 Amazon reviews (4.7-star average)
http://tinyurl.com/SleepingReviews

James Nixon

Other Books by James Nixon

THE CRASH OF MH370
(Recently Retired A380 Airline Captain
Explores the Mystery of the Doomed Airliner)

by

James Nixon

The Crash Of MH370 may well be one those ground breaking accidents that change our way of thinking. This book is an analysis of the mystery that is the missing Malaysian Airlines 777, and one of the first to be published after the search concluded.

Unlike previous books about the ghost plane written by well-meaning amateur pilots and journalists, the author is an industry insider; an A380 captain with similar experience to the missing Captain.

It examines the facts, who's who, the flight and search. The latter half dispels the various theories, provides the author's best guess as to what happened and delivers a list of thirteen urgent recommendations for the industry.

Rarely do we hear from people within this industry. From pilots and air traffic controllers to crash investigators, their employment contracts stipulate: *no media.*

That James Nixon has chosen to release this book within three months of his retirement means we are given a rare chance to peek behind the cockpit door.

Go to the Amazon site for the eBook & paperback:
http://tinyurl.com/CrashMH370

Also available at your local bookstore
(They may have to order it in for you)

Australian readers can order the paperback, saving both time and money:
www.JamesNixonBooks.com

or visit

Www.TheCrashOfMH370.com

Reader Reviews

THE CRASH OF MH370
(Recently Retired A380 Airline Captain
Explores the Mystery of the Doomed Airliner)

Informative, concise, and excellently-written

'A satisfying, concise yet detailed and well-written work about the unclear and mysterious circumstances of the MH370 tragedy. James has a unique combination of 30 years of pilot experience and great storytelling and writing skills, making for an unlikely thrilling read. He writes about complicated tech stuff with easy grace, empathy for the victims, optimistic that we must understand this story so it doesn't happen again. A rare and unexpected find in popular tech writing, right up there with Richard Feynman and Carl Sagan.'

M.Gurvits

***

Great Perspective, Easy Read

'The reviews already written state: great perspective, easy read, no hysteria, professional analysis, well written, minimum of jargon, satisfying, concise, detailed, great storytelling and writing skills, thrilling read, intelligent, factually examined, well balanced, informative. Yup … I agree with everything as stated. How can you improve on that? Five stars!'

Ray H

***

Credible and Commendable.
You will indeed
" learn stuff you've never heard before"

'As a former Airline pilot and Air Traffic Controller, I now read most MH370 analysis with skepticism. For the first time, I've found a review of the facts that raises no eyebrows. Don't mistake that for a book that is uninteresting - it's quite the opposite; in fact, this is the best aviation book I have read in several years. When James tells us *"Stick around; you're going to learn stuff you've never heard before"*, he's not kidding. There are countless gems of wisdom in here that every pilot and controller will find fascinating, and also, very useful in practical application. His theory of the reason for the incident is the most credible I've read. And his exoneration of the two pilots on this flight is not only justified, but highly commendable. James, thank you for writing this book.'

                Anonymous Amazon Reviewer

***

James Nixon

Excellent Read

'In The Crash of MH370, James Nixon has concisely and factually examined the greatest aviation mystery, bringing to bear more than 30 years as a pilot flying some of the most advanced and technical passenger aircraft ever built. When you want an expert opinion you ask someone with the experience of sitting on the flight deck for a living and someone who understands the technical and human aspects facing pilots today.

Far too many books have been written about MH370 by well-meaning overnight armchair experts, and conspiracy theorists looking to sow the seeds of their latest political, cultural hang-ups, and fantasy plots for the next Tom Clancy novel. As an aviation journalist, I've read my share of books penned by people who woke up one Saturday morning in 2014 and magically knew the difference between an APU and an SUV.

From the outset of this book, Nixon reminds his readers that the simplest explanation to an air crash is often the one closest to the truth and that there is always the danger to attribute what we don't understand to the nefarious or elaborate theories and scenarios.

Working through a number of theories, he presents his own opinion and theory on MH370 and 13 recommendations the industry should examine and implement.

An excellent read if you really want to cut through the misinformation and BS written about MH370.

Let's search on. The aviation industry needs it, and the flying public; but there are also 239 souls who deserve it at the very least.'

Mick Rooney
Aviation journalist
www.mh370investigation.com

Read the 62 Amazon reviews
(4.7-star average)
http://tinyurl.com/CrashReviews

James Nixon

Notes About Endnotes

Each link has been tested and will take you to the external website or Youtube video.

We can't guarantee the sites will not be removed at any time in the future, nor can we guarantee the legality of the copyright of each link.

If you notice that the links are broken, please take the time to email us so we can rectify the files for future readers:

Kerryn@CrammondMedia.com

1
"For Fear of Flying, Therapy Takes to the Skies"
TIM MURPHY   JULY 24, 2007 New York Times
http://www.nytimes.com/2007/07/24/health/psychology/24fear.html

2
**"The Holmes and Rahe Stress Scale
 Understanding the Impact of Long-term Stress"**
Mindtools.com website
https://www.mindtools.com/pages/article/newTCS_82.htm.

3
MedAire's Medlink
http://www.medaire.com/

4
Inter-Tropical Convergence Zone
National Weather Service definition:
http://www.srh.noaa.gov/jetstream/tropics/itcz.html

5
International Air Transport Association (IATA)
http://www.iata.org/Pages/default.aspx

6
Hibermate.com
https://www.hibermate.com/

7
PriorityPass
https://www.prioritypass.com/

8
Lounge Pass
https://www.loungepass.com/index.cfm?c=2

9
Lounge Club
https://www.loungeclub.com/en/

10
> **Guide To Sleeping In Airports**
> http://www.sleepinginairports.net/

11
> **SeatGuru.com**
> https://www.seatguru.com/

12
> **Audible.com**
> http://www.audible.com/

13
> **Sennheiser Ear Buds**
> https://en-us.sennheiser.com/earbuds-in-ear-headphones

14
> **Principles Of Flight**
> Video presentation by MIT Engineering
> https://www.youtube.com/watch?v=aLJzEl5st8s

15
> **"Flying Tiare - French Polynesia with a Go Pro
>   - Air Tahiti Nui"**
> One of the most spectacular videos of flying from a pilot's perspective.
> https://www.youtube.com/watch?v=P7EP9Ko6IsY

16
> **WhatsApp**
> https://www.whatsapp.com/

17
> **Hypoxia simulator test, "Hell of a way to die".**
> https://www.youtube.com/watch?v=XcvkjfG4A_M

18
> **Evernote.com**
> https://evernote.com/

19
DropBox.com
https://www.dropbox.com/

20
Packing Tips
https://www.youtube.com/watch?v=LIk8v__Osm8

www.ingramcontent.com/pod-product-compliance
Lightning Source LLC
Chambersburg PA
CBHW021129300426
44113CB00006B/358